Dedication

To every mother walking through every season— may you be sustained by His Word, steadied in the waiting, and surrounded by hope that never fades. This journey is sacred, and you are deeply loved.

Welcome, dear sister in Christ,

Motherhood is a journey like no other-filled with joy, challenge, love, and sometimes overwhelming moments. Whether you are expecting, healing, grieving, or embracing a unique path, this journal is designed to walk alongside you.

Rooted in Grace invites you to pause, breathe deeply, and anchor your heart in God's Word. Each chapter offers scripture, reflection, prayer, and journaling prompts to help you find strength and peace through every season of motherhood. This guide is not about perfection—it's about presence, grace, and the sacred invitation to lean into God's love even when life feels heavy. May you be encouraged, uplifted, and deeply rooted in the One who sustains you.

With love and prayers,
Gabrielle Bankston

Table of Contents

A Holy Beginning
For Expecting Mothers

Verse 1: Psalm 139:13-14 (NIV)
"For you created my inmost being; you knit me together in my mother's womb. I praise you because I am fearfully and wonderfully made; your works are wonderful…"

Devotional

The waiting is holy. Your body is a sacred vessel carrying life, and God is weaving His perfect plan within you. In moments of worry or fear, lean into His peace. You are not alone, and your baby is fearfully and wonderfully made.

Reflection Questions

What worries can I hand over to God today?

How can I embrace this season of waiting with hope?

Prayer

God, thank You for this precious life growing inside me.

Help me to trust Your timing and Your care. Fill me with peace and joy as I prepare to welcome this gift.

Journal Prompt

Today I feel _____ about this pregnancy.
God is reminding me that even when I feel
_____, He is _____.

Letter to Self

Verse 2: Proverbs 3:5–6 (NIV)
"Trust in the Lord with all your heart and lean not on your
own understanding..."

Devotional

Motherhood begins with trust—even before the first cry.
You may not understand what's happening in your body
or your emotions. But God invites you to lean on Him—
not on clarity, not on control. He promises to make your
path straight—even when you feel unsure.

Reflect:

Where am I trying to control instead of trust?

What would it look like to fully lean into God's strength today?

Prayer:

God, I surrender the parts I can't figure out.
Help me lean into You—not into my fears or logic.
Lead me as I carry this child and become the mom You've called me to be.

Journal Prompt:

Lately, I've been tryingto control_____.
But today, I choose to trust You with _____.

Letter to Self

Verse 3: Isaiah 41:10 (CSB)
"Do not fear, for I am with you; do not be afraid,
for I am your God..."

Devotional

You don't have to carry this alone.
Not the fears, not the pressure, not the "what ifs."
God is with you, in the quiet moments and the chaotic
ones.
He will strengthen you—not just on the delivery day,
but today, tomorrow, and every day after.

Reflect:

What fears keep showing up during this pregnancy?

What would change if I fully believed God was with me?

Prayer

Lord, quiet my fears. Be my steady presence.
Strengthen my heart when I feel unsure.
Thank You for never leaving my side—through every
stage of motherhood

Journal Prompt

Lately, I've been afraid of_____.
But I know God is with me, and He promises to
_____.

Letter to Self

....

....

....

....

....

....

....

Verse 4: Jeremiah 1:5 (ESV)
"Before I formed you in the womb I knew you..."

Devotional

You're not just carrying a baby—you're carrying purpose
before anyone knew this child existed, God did.
He already has a plan, a calling, and a future for them.
And that same God is walking with you.
Nothing about this pregnancy surprises Him. He chose
you for this.

Reflect

How does it feel to know God already knows and loves my child?

In what ways am I being prepared for this calling?

Prayer

Thank You, God, for choosing me to carry this child.
Even when I feel unsure or undeserving,
You remind me that I am chosen and equipped.
Let me rest in Your perfect plan for both of us.

Journal Prompt

God chose me for this child because_ _____.

I'm learning that I don't need to be perfect—
I just need to _____.

Letter to Self

Healing After Birth

For the mother piecing herself back together while holding someone else together.

Verse 1: Isaiah 66:13 (NIV) "As a mother comforts her child, so will I comfort you; and you will becomforted..."

Devotional

You are the comforter now—but you also need comfort. Postpartum can feel like a storm of emotion, fatigue, and unfamiliar change.
But God does not leave mothers out of His gentleness. Just as you rock your baby, He rocks you in His arms. He is with you in the tears, the stitches, the silence, the swirl of hormones. You are not weak—you are human, and holy, and healing. Let Him meet you there.

Reflection Questions

Where in my body or heart do I feel most
tender today?

How has God shown up in small ways during this
healing time?

Prayer

God, thank You for being close to me as I recover.
I've given so much—I need You to pour back into me.
Surround me with Your comfort.
Heal what no one sees. Calm what I can't explain.
Thank You for never growing tired of holding me.

Journal Prompt

Right now, I feel _____ physically.
Emotionally, I've been _____, and
I need God to _____.

Letter to Self

_____

_____

_____

_____

_____

_____

_____

Verse 2: Psalm 147:3 (NLT)
"He heals the broken hearted and bandages their wounds."

Devotional

Healing is not just for visible wounds.
Whether you're recovering from a tough delivery, a traumatic birth, or expectations that didn't match reality—God sees it all.
He does not rush your process.
You don't have to be strong all the time.
You are allowed to grieve what didn't go as planned, even as you celebrate what did.

Reflection

What part of my story have I been afraid to talk about?

Is there something I need to grieve in order to heal?

Prayer

Lord, I give You the parts of my story that still ache.
Heal me gently. Heal me fully.
Help me remember that my softness is not weakness—
it's sacred.

Journal Prompt

One part of my story I haven't shared is _____
But I know God sees it, and He is _____.

Letter to Self

Verse 3: Matthew 11:28 (NIV)
"Come to me, all you who are weary
and burdened, and I will give you rest."

Devotional

You don't have to earn rest. You don't have to wait
until the laundry's done or until your body is "back.
" Jesus invites you into rest today. Even 5 minutes with
Him can reset your soul.

Let go of the guilt. Let yourself be loved—fully,
tenderly, endlessly.

Reflection Questions

What's weighing on me right now that I haven't brought to God?

Where can I create space to rest, even in the middle of motherhood?

Prayer

Jesus, I am tired.
Tired in my body, my heart, and my mind.
Help me pause. Help me breathe.
Help me remember that I don't have to hold
everything —because You already are.

Journal Prompt

Lately, I've been carrying_____.
But God is offering me _____ in return.

Letter to Self

....

....

....

....

....

....

....

....

Verse 4: 2 Corinthians 4:16 (NIV)
"Though outwardly we are wasting away, yet inwardly we are being renewed day by day."

Devotional

Your body may feel worn. Your emotions may feel stretched thin. But God is doing a quiet, sacred work inside you. Renewal doesn't always look like energy—it can look like grace. It can look like a deep breath, a kind thought toward yourself, a moment of peace in the chaos.

You are not just recovering—you are being remade. Day by day, He is restoring your strength, your spirit, your sense of self. Let that truth settle into your bones.

Reflection

What does "renewal" look like for me today—physically, emotionally, spiritually?

Where have I seen glimpses of God rebuilding me, even in small ways?

Prayer

God, thank You for renewing me even when I feel undone. Help me notice the quiet ways You're rebuilding me. Give me patience with the process. Let Your grace be the rhythm I walk to—slow, steady, and full of hope.

Journal Prompt

I've felt worn out by _____, but
I've also noticed God renewing me through
_____.

Letter to Self

The Long Nights, the Little Years

For the tired mom who wishes time would slow down.

Verse 1: Galatians 6:9 (NLT)

"So, let's not get tired of doing what is good.
At just the right time we will reap a harvest
of blessing if we don't give up."

Devotional

You're doing holy work—even at 3 a.m., teeth
unbrushed, thoughts drowned out by toys.
The world may not see diaper changes and
tear-wiping as ministry.
— but God does.
He sees your invisible faithfulness.
He sees how you choose love again and again.
He promises this season—yes, even this one
—holds eternal harvest.

Reflection

What part of this season feels the most exhausting?

What might God be growing in me through this daily work?

Prayer

Lord, I feel like I'm running on empty.

Remind me that this work is holy, even when it feels ordinary.

Help me see my child—and myself—the way You do: worth the effort, worth the love, worth showing up for.

Journal Prompt

Right now I feel _____ in this season.
But I believe God is growing _____ in me.

Letter to Self

Verse 2: Ecclesiastes 3:1, 4 (CSB)
"There is a time for everything... a time to weep and a time to laugh, a time to mourn and a time to dance."

Devotional

The days are long, but the years are short.
You laugh while you cry.
You miss the cuddles before they're even gone.
You feel guilty for wishing for rest—and then guilty again for wanting more time.
This is the in-between season, and it's allowed to be both beautiful and hard.
God honors your tears and your giggles.
He walks with you through every "last first."

Reflection

What do I miss already, even as I live
it?

How can I allow myself to fully feel this season
without rushing through it?

Prayer

Jesus, help me stop rushing and start noticing.
Give me eyes to see the holy moments in the middle of
the mess.
Help me hold space for both joy and exhaustion.

Journal Prompt

Lately I've been rushing through _____,
but God is inviting me to slow down and see

_____.

Letter to Self

Verse 3: Psalm 121:3-4 (ESV)
"He who keeps you will not slumber. Behold, he who keeps Israel will neither slumber nor sleep."

Devotional

You are not alone in the night.
God doesn't sleep through your motherhood.
He is awake when you are.
He sees the bottles, the pacing, the shushing, the rocking.
And when your eyes can barely stay open, He is still holding you.

Reflection

What do I most need from God when I'm awake at night?

Have I been trying to carry this alone?

Prayer

God, thank You for staying awake with me.
When I am overwhelmed, remind me that I am not alone.
Let Your peace hold my heart, even when my arms are full.

Journal Prompt

When I'm awake at night, I often feel _____.
But God is near, and He is _____.

Letter to Self

Verse 4: Isaiah 40:11 (NIV)
"He tends his flock like a shepherd:
He gathers the lambs in his arms
and carries them close to his heart;
He gently leads those that have young."

Devotional

You are not forgotten in the crowd. God sees the mother with her hands full and her heart stretched thin. He doesn't rush you. He doesn't shame your weariness. He gathers you close—yes, you—and leads you gently. You don't have to be strong all the time. You just have to be held.

Reflection

Where have I felt carried by God lately?

What does "gentle leading" look like in my motherhood?

Prayer

Lord, thank You for being a gentle Shepherd. Lead me with kindness when I feel overwhelmed. Help me rest in Your arms, even when I'm still moving.

Journal

I've been trying to carry _____ alone, but God is gently leading me toward _____.

Letter to Self

....

....

....

....

....

....

....

....

When You're Doing It Alone

For the mother carrying strength and tenderness all by herself.

Verse 1: Psalm 68:5-6 (NIV)

"A father to the fatherless, a defender of widows, is God in his holy dwelling. God sets the lonely in families…"

Devotional

You were never meant to carry this alone—yet you keep showing up. You pour out when no one's pouring into you but sweet friend, God sees you.
He steps into your exhaustion.
He's not just Father to your child—He's Father to you.
You are never abandoned, never unseen, never unloved.

Reflection

Where do I feel most unsupported in this season?

How has God shown up as my support when no one else did?

Prayer

God, I feel the weight of doing it all.
Some days I don't know if I can keep going.
But You are near.
You defend me, lift me, comfort me.
Remind me I'm not mothering alone—you are here,
always.

Journal Prompt

Lately, I've felt alone in _____.
But I believe God is showing me _____.

Letter to Self

Verse 2: Isaiah 41:10 (NLT)

"Don't be afraid, for I am with you. Don't be discouraged, for I am your God.
I will strengthen you and help you. I will hold you up..."

Devotional

You don't have to be strong all the time.
You can cry in the car, scream into your pillow, sit in the silence—and still be a good mom.
God's strength is made perfect in your weakness.
When your knees buckle under the pressure, His hands hold you up.
You may feel alone, but He is whispering, "I'm still here. I've never left."

Reflection

What have I been trying to carry by myself?

What do I need to surrender to God's strength today?

Prayer

Lord, I need You to hold me together.
Remind me I don't have to carry the world alone.
Thank You for strengthening me when I feel empty.

Journal

I've been trying to carry _____ on my own.
But today I give it to God, and I trust Him to

_____.

Letter to Self

Verse 3: Lamentations 3:22–23 (ESV)
"The steadfast love of the Lord never ceases; His mercies never come to an end; they are new every morning…"

Devotional

Every day you wake up, you get a new mercy.
Not yesterday's mercy. Not tomorrow's strength.
Today's portion, for today's pain. And that's enough.
You may not have the help you wish for,
but you have a God who never runs out of love,
never stops showing up and never grows tired of your
prayers.

Reflection

What does "new mercy" look like for me today?

How can I begin to trust that what God gives is enough for this day?

Prayer

God, I'm thankful that I don't have to live off yesterday's grace. Give me today's mercy, today's strength, and today's peace. Let me breathe, knowing You're not asking me to be perfect— just present.

Journal

Today's mercy looks like _____. God is not asking me to _____, but instead to _____.

Letter to Self

Verse 4: Matthew 11:28–30 (NIV)
"Come to me, all you who are weary and burdened,
and I will give you rest.
Take my yoke upon you and learn from me, for I am gentle
and humble in heart, and you will find rest for your souls.
For my yoke is easy and my burden is light."

Devotional

You weren't meant to carry this alone. Not the late-night
worries. Not the endless decisions.
Not the ache of doing it all. Jesus sees your weariness and
doesn't ask you to push through—He invites you to rest.
Not just sleep, but soul-deep restoration. He is gentle with
your heart, patient with your healing, and present in your
overwhelm.
You don't have to earn His help. You only have to come.
Lay down the burden. Let Him carry you.

Reflection

What burdens am I carrying that God never asked me to?

What would it look like to truly rest in Jesus today?

Prayer

Jesus, I'm tired. Not just in my body, but in my spirit. Teach me how to rest in You. Help me release the pressure and receive Your peace. Let Your gentleness quiet my striving, and Your love carry me through.

Journal

I've been trying to keep up with _____. But God is inviting me to slow down and trust Him with _____.

Letter to Self

....

....

....

....

....

....

....

Grieving in Silence

For the mother carrying unspoken sorrow and hidden tears.

Verse 1: Psalm 34:18 (NIV)
"The Lord is close to the brokenhearted and saves those who are crushed in spirit."

Devotional

Grief is heavy, and it often arrives without warning. It whispers in quiet moments, hides behind smiles, and lingers where no one else looks. God sees the depths of your broken heart. He is not distant or detached—He draws near to you in the shadows. You don't have to pretend or hide your pain from Him. In your sorrow, He is your closest companion.

Reflection

Where in my heart am I feeling broken or crushed right now?

How can I invite God's closeness into my grief today?

Prayer

Lord, I am hurting in places words cannot reach.
Come close to me and hold my shattered heart.
Help me find peace even in my pain.
Thank You for never leaving me alone in this darkness.

Journal

My grief feels like _____.
Today, I will invite God to _____.

Letter to Self

....

....

....

....

....

....

....

Verse 2: Matthew 5:4 (ESV)
"Blessed are those who mourn, for they shall be comforted."

Devotional

Your mourning is sacred.

There is blessing in your tears—tears that cleanse, heal, and eventually transform.

God honors your mourning because it means you love deeply.

You don't have to rush past your grief or put it on a timeline.

Your heart's healing is a process held tenderly in God's hands.

Reflection

What part of my loss do I need to mourn
fully?

How might God be comforting me right now, even if I
don't feel it yet?

Prayer

God, I give You my mourning heart.
Comfort me as only You can.
Teach me to trust Your timing and rest in Your love.

Journal Prompt

I mourn_____ today.

I trust God to _____ in His perfect time.

Letter to Self

Verse 3: Revelation 21:4 (NIV)
"He will wipe every tear from their eyes.
There will be no more death or mourning or crying or
pain..."

Devotional

Oneday, all grief will end.
All tears will be wiped away, and pain will be no more.
Until then, God holds your tears and carries your pain.
Your grief is not wasted—
it is sacred soil where new hope will grow. Hold onto
this promise: your sorrow is temporary, but God's love
is eternal.

Reflection

How does the promise of no more pain give me hope today?

What small seeds of hope can I nurture in my grieving heart?

Prayer

Thank You, God, for the hope that outshines my sorrow.
Help me hold onto Your promises when grief feels
overwhelming. Fill me with peace and anticipation
for the day You make all things new.

Journal

Today, my hope is_____.
God's promise gives me strength to _____.

Letter to Self

Verse 4: Isaiah 53:3–4 (NIV)

"He was despised and rejected by mankind, a man of suffering, and familiar with pain... Surely he took up our pain and bore our suffering..."

Devotional

Jesus knows grief—not just in theory, but in experience. He carried sorrow in His body, rejection in His heart, and pain in His soul.

You are not alone in your silent suffering. He doesn't just understand your tears—He shares them.

When no one else sees the weight you carry, He does. And He doesn't turn away. He draws near, takes up your pain, and whispers, "I'm with you in this." Your grief is not too heavy for Him.

Reflection

What part of my grief feels too heavy to share with anyone?

How does knowing Jesus is familiar with sorrow comfort me today?

Prayer

Jesus, You know what it means to suffer. You've felt rejection, loneliness, and deep sorrow.
Help me trust that You understand my pain.
Lift the weight I've been carrying in silence. Let Your presence be my comfort and my healing.

Journal

The part of my grief I've kept hidden is
_____. But today, I let Jesus carry _____
with me.

Letter to Self

....

....

....

....

....

....

....

....

Walking a Different Path

For the mother embracing a unique journey with her child.

Verse 1: Psalm 139:14 (NIV)
"I praise you because I am fearfully
and wonderfully made; your works are wonderful, I know
that full well."

Devotional

Your child is wonderfully made—unique, precious, and perfectly
designed by God.
Though the path may look different than you expected, it is no
less holy.
God's creativity shines in every special need, every different
ability.
You are walking a brave path filled with love, challenges, and
endless grace.
You are not alone—God is with you every step.

Reflection

How can I celebrate the unique giftsin my child and myself?

Where have I seen God's handiwork in our journey?

Prayer

Lord, thank You for making my child fearfully and wonderfully.

Help me to see beauty in our different path and to trust Your plan.

Give me strength and joy for each step we take together

Journal

I am grateful for _____in our unique journey.
God's love shows up when _____.

Letter to Self

Verse 2: 2 Corinthians 12:9 (NIV)
"My grace is sufficient for you, for my power is made perfect in weakness."

Devotional

You don't have to have all the answers or be perfect.
God's grace covers every moment of weakness, every exhausted tear, every unknown tomorrow. In your moments of doubt or struggle,
His power shines brightest.
You are not defined by challenges but by the strength God provides daily.

Reflection Questions

What weaknesses or struggles am I offering to God today?

How have I experienced His grace in tough moments?

Prayer

God, Your grace is enough for me today.
Fill me with Your strength when I feel weak.
Help me to rest in Your power and love.

Journal Prompt

Today I surrender _____ to God's grace.
I trust that He will _____ in my weakness.

Letter to Self

....

....

....

....

....

....

....

Verse 3: Romans 8:28 (NIV)
"And we know that in all things
God works for the good of those who love him..."

Devotional

Even when the road is hard and full of unknowns,
God is working behind the scenes. He is weaving
purpose, healing, and hope into your story. Your love
for your child and your faith in God creates a powerful
story of resilience. Trust that He is making beauty
from the challenges.

Reflection

What "good" might God be working in our journey,
even if I can't see it yet?

How can I hold onto hope through uncertainty?

Prayer

Thank You, God, that You work all things for good.
Help me trust You when I can't see the full picture.
Fill me with hope and peace in every step of this unique
path.

Journal

I believe God is working good in
_____. Today, I choose hope by
_____.

Letter to Self

Verse 4: John 9:2–3 (NIV)
"Rabbi, who sinned, this man or his parents,
that he was born blind?' 'Neither this man nor his
parents sinned,' said Jesus,
'but this happened so that the works of God might be
displayed in him."

Devotional

Your story is not a mistake. Your child's story is not a punishment. Jesus silences shame and replaces it with purpose. Disability is not a detour—it's a canvas for God's glory. In every limitation, He paints strength. In every challenge, He reveals beauty. You and your child are living testimonies of grace, resilience, and divine design. God's works are being displayed in both of you —every single day.

Reflection

Where have I felt shame or judgment in our journey?

How is God displaying His glory through our lives?

Prayer

Jesus, thank You for seeing us with love, not labels.
Silence the voices of shame and
replace them with Your truth.
Let Your glory shine through our story—through every challenge, every triumph, every quiet moment of grace.

Journal Prompt

God is displaying His glory in_____.
Even when others don't understand, I will choose to

_____.

Letter to Self

··

··

··

··

··

··

··

··

Closing the Chapter

For the mother holding her last baby, feeling the mix of joy and goodbye.

Verse 1: Ecclesiastes 3:1 (NIV)
"There is a time for everything, and a season for every activity under the heavens..."

Devotional

Motherhood is full of seasons—some that stretch long and others that pass in the blink of an eye. Holding your last child brings a tender mix of celebration and farewell. God's timing is perfect, and every season has purpose. It's okay to feel both grateful and grief all at once. He walks with you through every ending and new beginning.

Reflection

What emotions am I feeling as I hold this final season?

How can I lean on God's timing and trust in His plan?

Prayer

Lord, thank You for every moment, every memory,
every milestone. Help me embrace this season with
open hands and a trusting heart. Give me peace as
I say goodbye to one chapter and welcome what's next.

Journal

I feel _____ as I close this chapter.
God's timing teaches me _____.

Letter to Self

....

....

....

....

....

....

....

....

Verse 2: Isaiah43:18-19 (NIV)
"Forget the former things; do not dwell on the past.
See, I am doing a new thing! Now it springs up; do you
not perceive it?"

Devotional

Closing a chapter doesn't mean forgetting—it means making space for what's next. God invites you to release what was and embrace what He's doing now. There is a newness, a fresh hope, waiting for you beyond the familiar. Even in endings, God's grace writes beautiful beginnings.

Reflection

What past moments do I need to release to move forward?

What new thing might God be inviting me to notice today?

Prayer

God, help me let go of what's behind and trust You with what's ahead.

Open my eyes to the new things You're doing in my life. Fill me with hope and courage for this next season.

Journal Prompt

I am ready to release _____ and welcome
_____. God's new thing in my life is
_____.

Letter to Self

Verse 3: Philippians 3:13-14 (NIV)
"Forgetting what is behind and straining toward what is ahead, I press on toward the goal to win the prize..."

Devotional

Life moves forward—sometimes faster than we want.
God calls you to keep pressing on, not by forgetting your story, but by holding it lightly.
Your motherhood journey is a beautiful story that continues beyond baby years.
He strengthens you to run the race ahead with hope, joy, and grace.

Reflection

How can I honor my past while moving forward
with hope?

What "prize" or goal is God encouraging me to press
toward now?

Prayer

Lord, help me press on with joy and purpose.
Thank You for the journey and the strength to keep going.
Lead me forward into the blessings You have prepared.

Journal

I honor my past by_____.
Today, I choose to press forward by _____.

Letter to Self

....

....

....

....

....

....

....

Verse 4: Psalm 126:5 (NIV)
"Those who sow with tears will reap with songs of joy."

Devotional

This season may be sown with tears—of gratitude, of letting go, of deep love. But God promises joy on the other side of surrender.

You've poured out your heart in the sacred work of motherhood, and He sees every seed planted. The laughter, the prayers, the sleepless nights— they've watered a legacy of faith.

Now, as you close this chapter, joy begins to rise—not because it's easy, but because
He is faithful.

Reflection

What seeds have I sown in this season that I hope will bloom in my child's life?

How can I trust that God will turn my tears into joy?

Prayer

Lord, Thank You for the tears that have watered this season.
Let joy rise in me as I trust You with the harvest.
May my motherhood be a song of praise to Your goodness.

Journal Prompt

I've sown _____ in love and faith. I trust God to bring joy through _____.

Letter to Self

Affirmations

I am held by grace, even when I feel stretched thin.

God's love flows through me as I nurture and guide.

I am not alone—He walks with me through every season.

My imperfections are invitations for His strength to shine.

I am rooted in faith, not shaken by fear or comparison.

Peace is mine, not because life is easy, but because He is near.

I am equipped for this calling—grace is my daily provision.

My motherhood is a ministry, sacred and divinely appointed.

I release the need to do it all and rest in His sufficiency.

The love I give echoes in eternity—He multiplies every seed.